This book is to be returned on or before
the last date stamped below.

2 MAY 2002

16 MAY 2002

LODOLA

LODOLA

with texts by
Aldo Busi
Laura Cherubini
Sam Hunter

Electa

Marco Lodola
Inner City Lights
Marisa Del Re Gallery
New York

Press Office
Centro italiano per le arti e la cultura,
Turin-Rome
Delos, Milan
Cristine Paulve, Paris

Photographs
Vittorio Dozio
Piercarlo Invernizzi

Portrait Photograph
Francesco Illy

Translation
Jeremy Scott

Thanks go to
Bone Machine, Stefano Carlissi,
Sara De Michele, Cristina Garbagna,
Edoardo Lomuoio, Neon Pavia,
Luciano Paladini, Claudio Poleschi,
Anna Piccarreta, Waifro Spaggiari,
Gail Swerling, Dario Tagliabue, Timoria

Contents

Untitled, 1997
Pencil and ink on paper, 24 x 33 cm

Introduction

Sam Hunter

His apparently unlimited variety of dancing figures bring references to the choreography and now-neglected hedonism of classical musicals together with other, sometimes grimmer, associations. His faceless Everyman and Everywoman are sometimes involved in scenes of anonymous madness, with echoes of social violence and even revolution. Then, with easy changes of mood and reference, Lodola shifts his disconnected and multiple icon of Man of the Masses into a network of purely formal references, sometimes including a "Cascade" of colored rectangles which can be interpreted as standards and pennants or as simple colored rectangles. Or perhaps they are "standards of the abstract"—that is, of a form of expression now seen as a lost cause (or, at the very least, as one that is drained of inspiration).

It is this facility in shifting ground which eliminates the apparent superficiality of Lodola's roughly modeled plastic forms and, together with their iconographical accessibility, enables them to open whole new scenarios in the mass-media culture that inspired them. While his prolific and apparently carefree output reveals an essentially lyrical style, it is nevertheless true that Lodola adopts a much more intellectual and satirical approach than those artists he has taken as models—foremost among whom there is Larry Rivers, whose rather romantic outlines of a dancing Fred Astaire (produced at the end of the 1980s) could have been a model for Lodola. Ironically, Rivers' numerous variations on the theme of "the dancer" were in part inspired by the kinetic experiments with the dynamics of movement that were part of Futurism and Vorticism. Undoubtedly, Lodola would immediately deny any link with such "elevated" culture; and perhaps his real affinity is with the much more accessible and culturally primitive work of Keith Haring, creator of the "radiant child."

But whatever stream in American art you link Lodola with, his work has its own energy, lucidity and range of invention—together with a European breadth of reference. What is more, there is an implicitly rather grim social content which occasionally makes itself plain, communicating a real feeling of uneasiness in the midst of visual pleasure. With growing awareness and distress, we are his accomplices as we briefly lower ourselves into the swamp of mass culture.

Silhouettes in Silhouette

Aldo Busi

I have owned two of Lodola's plastic silhouettes for years, but I am never quite sure how to set them up; sometimes I'm not even sure how I should look at them. They remind me of the figures that one of my primary school teachers used to cut out of hardboard using a fretsaw; carefully finished off in oil paints, these were given as prizes to the best—or best-behaved—pupils (so that, in the end, there was always one for everyone, even the worst, and the worst-behaved). These figures depicted tropical fish, dwarfs, renowned fairy-tale queens, small houses with a little dog , and even coral and strands of seaweed—a true feast for the eyes, something each one of us wanted for our very own. Unlike Lodola's work, the figures produced by my primary school teacher had a base; they stood up on their own, so there was no need to prop them up against something—and certainly the attempt to give them the correct equilibrium in space didn't bother you that much, nor for very long (given their size you could have gotten half a dozen of them on the cover of a schoolbook). However—to mention just one of a whole range of figures—Lodola's near-life-size dancing girls don't always stay in place when you prop them up against a wall; you never know which way they are going to fall, and you soon get used to the fact that you can't impose your own point of view on them. They have their own point of view, which is often capricious and, let's be honest, obstinate, outrageous, *feminine*: artistic. After a few days they start giving you such looks that you know they want to be moved from where you've put them; from the sitting-room they go into the kitchen, from the kitchen to the bathroom. You even try to hang them up from a nail; but you need a least three nails if you are going to give them a reasonably life-like pose. So you bang in the three nails, only to find that her hip knocks one of them out, and she ends up head-over-tutu. You leave her like that for a week—to teach her a lesson; hoping that with all that plastic running to her head she'll soon adopt her own eternal—and very special—dancestep. But one day you get home and find that she is leaning wildly to the right, just hanging on by the one remaining nail, and clearly determined that she be given another move. So there she is, attached to you, unwilling to let you go, wanting to experience that secret theater of your own emptiness in movement. Crazy things like that.

Of course, the lamps are a totally different matter. They are much more obedient to their master and his own requirements in matters of interior design, to his changes of mind, his

moments of visual boredom. Having seen them, I can guarantee that at least they stand up, and that they stay where you put them in the way you arranged them. And nowadays something that stands up on its own two feet is not to be sneezed at. Indeed, it is positively splendid. But, living with them must be very different from just walking around them. Do you leave them switched on all the time? Turn them on only when you have guests? Use them instead of the normal light fittings? And if it fails, what do you do? Call the restorer, a blacksmith, an electrician, a gallery-owner—or Lodola himself? Total short circuit!

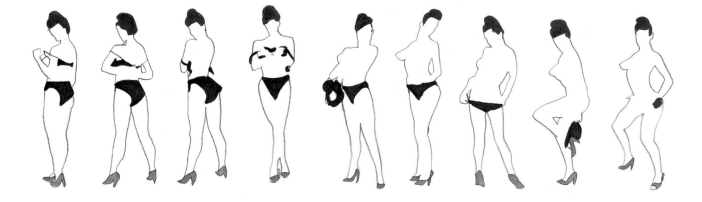

Variety Show

Laura Cherubini

A publicity shot for the 1929 film *Broadway Melody* shows three girls in "short" costumes (the sort that might be described as "succinct" in a police report). Bejeweled and be-lipsticked, they totter on high heels while holding up letters which spell out the film's title. A mix of dancing, songs and comic sketches, this was one of the first musicals to obtain an Oscar—it also seems to me to be the perfect introduction to Marco Lodola's work, a sort of visual manifesto containing all the elements which form the basis of his art: musicals and their inexhaustible supply of images and pirouettes; dance in general; neon signs (a typical component of urban iconography); the outline (an empty perimeter, a container of nothing, an abstract silhouette that goes blank once you move inside it); the arrangement of a pose, or rather the fleeting instant of a pose.

Shall We Dance
"So, what is a musical? It is quite simply a film built around music. Its own music, its own songs. Take away the musical notes and the film ceases to exist" (Lee Edward Stern). But that turns out to be untrue. Marco Lodola has shown that the play of forms in a musical can replace the playing of music. It was in 1933 that Busby Berkeley took the first steps towards earning himself of the title "King of Choreography" with abstract kaleidoscopic dance routines for three fantastic films: *Gold Diggers of 1933*, *42nd Street* and *Footlight Parade* (the first directed by Mervin LeRoy, the other two by Lloyd Bacon). "A designer rather than a choreographer, he showed himself to be uninhibited by tradition, conventions or even questions of good taste. His film camera moved everywhere, in the middle of everything; it shot things from above, from below, through transparent floors, through water. It was the camera which created the dance. People and pianos, revolving doors and cascades of water, were all just moving parts of an enormous choreographical puzzle, of attractive visual patterns that were continually forming and disintegrating on the screen," wrote Lee Edward Stern of Berkeley's choreography, an important component of which he sees as being "the element of surprise." His work on those films would stand Berkeley in good stead when over the next ten years he worked with Esther Williams and her girls on spectacular sequences of synchronized swimming.

While maintaining all the iconography of the musical, Marco Lodola undercuts its rules. He ignores the sound element to concentrate entirely on the visual. Rhythm and dance are a key element in musicals, but Lodola freezes all movement in complicated poses cut out of rigid perspex; and at the same time he renders homage to the anonymity of the chorus-line (while musicals themselves were to find their most harmonious expression in focus of one main actor/crowd puller—be it Fred Astaire, Gene Kelly, Ginger Rogers, Judy Garland or even the young Shirley Temple).

Lodola blocks the "element of surprise" by using one of the very methods that was used to obtain it: the mechanism of repetition. The artist works on this theme of reiteration and extracts from the musical the formal abstract principle on which it was based (a principle that appeared disguised as variety and variety numbers). With regard to this theme, Marisa

Vescovo has spoken of "a nostalgia that is disguised by means of formal geometry."
Musicals are based on the formal principle of continual repetition, which is an integral part
of the laws of vision. It is no coincidence that the work of the choreographer goes together with that of a set designer and a costume designer—all their efforts being dominated by
the principle of a symmetry that is continually broken up and reestablished by the unend-
ing twists and turns of the dance.

In the chorus-line scenes all the dancers are dressed alike, as if they were all versions of one
single woman. Even more striking is one particular scene in *Shall We Dance:* Fred Astaire
searches out a Ginger Rogers (he would perhaps quite willingly have done without) from
among a whole crowd of girls wearing Ginger Rogers masks (all sporting a face which, as
they say, is as American as apple pie). In *Blue Skies*, on the other hand, Fred Astaire dances
alone, with reflections of himself in a number of mirrors. The mask and the mirror, symbols
of the image doubled and multiplied. Taking up the term from Deleuze, Renato Barilli has
spoken here of "differing repetition"—and this is precisely the aspect of musicals caught in
Marco Lodola's work. Dance has been known to man since his very origins; it is so much a
part of nature that there are even some animals which perform dances. And in Eastern phi-
losophy there is the theme of sacred ritual dance, of trances in which one loses oneself.
However, Lodola consciously mixes high and low culture in a post-modernist cocktail, so
this learned and spiritual theme is taken up using musicals, the most popular genre of the
most popular of artistic languages (cinema)—those very musicals that have now practical-
ly died out due to their high costs, the demise of the Big Studios and the ever-increasing

The *Gold Diggers
of 1933:* Berkeley's
dancers in a typical
configuration

power of the entertainment snippets provided by Madame TV. So,
it's Sunset Boulevard time for a genre that helped an entire gener-
ation of Americans get over the Great Depression: *42nd Street*, for
example, was a celebration of personal initiative and held up the figure of Warner Baxter as a leader—and one should not forget that
"part of the advertising campaign for the launch of the film involved
a lavish train, full of Warner Bros. stars (including Ginger Rogers),
traveling around the country to celebrate Roosevelt's election as
President" (Patrick McGilligan).

Puzzle

Another theme of "high" culture is that of the ultimate meaning of
life, of the true sense of that dialectic between individual and group
(an idea expressed by Aristotle's definition of man as a "political
animal"). Again Marco Lodola tackles this theme through a corre-
spondent idea in "low" culture, exploiting the "collective" effort that
is not only a feature of musicals but of dance as a whole (even classical ballet has rigid rules governing the movement of the corps de

ballet; in some ways the dancers are shifted around like little soldiers—perhaps this explains why such high levels of balletic excellence were achieved in the countries of East Europe). Scenes choreographed *en masse* lead to mass de-personalization; where the choreography and set design are at their most complicated, the dancers become abstract components of enormous human puzzles. The facial features of the individual disappear; there are no longer any details (be they details of costume or details of physical appearance).

Lodola's aim is to avoid the individually recognizable. The disappearance of distinctive traits means that everything can be copied, repeated. This is part of the reason for his choice of the theme of musicals—just as it lies behind the choice of the other popular genres he works with: punk, quiz shows, etc. Each one enables him to explore what is the dominant formal aspect of his art: the lack of recognition, the avoidance of identity, and hence the achievement of abstraction. However, Lodola's works are neither totally abstract nor totally figurative—or rather, they are both at one and the same

time (just as they are both painting and sculpture at one and the same time). The images are created through the use of colored outlines, forming figures that rely on the juxtaposition of chromatic fields, flat cut-outs of color. The use of white, on the other hand, serving to sublimate the carnality of the bodies, render them diaphanous.

Forms fit together like parts of a puzzle—a procedure that we are all familiar with (Barilli frequently emphasized the ludic element in "Nuovo Futurismo"—a movement of which he himself was the main critical voice and to which Lodola belonged in the early 1980s). Out of a mass of the most varied forms and unrecognizable details, an immediately identifiable image emerges. From fragmentation to unity, from the unidentifiable detail to something that is perceived clearly and distinctly. This is what happens in Lodola's work. We immediately capture the meaning of the scene, but if we break it down into its components, none of them are realistic or identifiable. It is identity that eludes us: the password that enables these figures to move from the world of celluloid to the space of art is "anonymity."

Transparency, Light, Shadow

But yet another link between the worlds of high and low culture emerges when we see that the principle behind the puzzles is taken from the history of art: Lodola's work making a clear reference to Matisse's *papiers découpés*. Matisse himself said that those cut-outs enabled him to "draw in color," and I would say that this is Lodola's aim as well when he cuts and paints plastic (an activity that seems to give him a great deal of pleasure). Lodola looks upon this favorite procedure of his as painting and certainly not as design. Another possible reference might be to the empty outlines cut out by the pop artist Tom Wesselmann (both of these references in Lodola's creations were perceptively caught by Elio Grazioli). However, quite apart from the recent works by Wesselmann, I would say that one could find another perfect "fit" with Lodola's works in the pop artist's earlier use of planes and outlines of color. Looking at Lodola's first works of 1981—the girl in net stockings in a red environment, or the youth in a colored jacket in a

blue room—the themes of his aesthetic research already seem clear, and we catch echoes of the early Wesselmann and of the Matisse of *The Red Studio* or *The Blue Window* (works in which the French artist constructed the pictorial space through repetitions of the same color with slight variations in tone and shade). In his works from the early eighties, using acrylic on canvas, Lodola painted clean, smooth areas of color, offering a clear foretaste of the later works of figures created in plastic.

His very choice of perspex as the Matter (not just the material) of his art is another result of Lodola's desire to bring together a traditional technique and a modern medium. As Roberto D'Agostino points out "the viewpoint here is that of plastic, the Grand Reproducer of Merchandise, which sees everything as a copy." The materials and methods aim for the

Top Hat, 1935, Fred and Ginger in "Cheek to Cheek"

same anonymity as that to be seen in the image itself; as George S. Bolge points out, any hint of the sensitive hand of the artist is repressed and even the use of industrial enamel paint contributes to this process of de-personalization.

One noteworthy characteristic of perspex is its transparency—the simultaneous dimension of depth and surface. Along with perspex, the recent works have involved the use of neon: transparency being a property of light, tending towards the state of light. While cutting plastic—perhaps the most revolutionary material of the twentieth century—allowed Lodola to "draw in color," the insertion of a neon framework within a translucid perspex shell makes it possible for him to "draw with light." The large totem entitled *Quiz Show* is a light machine that brings together the ancient theme of the obelisk and the most populist of modern television. For some time now we have all known that "life is a quiz" and "you at home make the program yourselves." So, by accident or bad luck, the last great collective product which subsumes a number of traditions—including the tradition of musicals—is television.

These works with light, these *light boxes*, are close relatives to the neon signs to be seen outside the bars and restaurants throughout our cities—the most recent expression of the practice of urban embellishment that, in the past, involved such great artists as Bernini. The works always have titles which evoke a multiplicity of references. In *Ode* the color red is dominant; this is a veritable symphony of color rather than sound, just as Matisse's *Red Studio* was a symphony of color. But now the reference to Matisse's color cut-outs raises another, more profound, theme that is basic to the work of both artists—the theme of dance. As always, the wheel has come full circle. The ethereal silhouette evokes images of the flow of poses that form dance. Indeed, after Busby Berkeley's futuristic kaleidoscopic choreographies, the musical went through a different phase, of which the most characteristic feature was the daring flow of steps achieved by the most fleet-footed couple in the world: Fred Astaire and Ginger Rogers, who formed a winged creature with two heads and four feet (like something out of a medieval bestiary). Lodola seems to oscillate between these two moments in the history of the musical: the choreography of the whole and the choreography of the acrobatic solo number.

Fruits moves on to another form of urban furnishing: the movie poster. In this case, it uses the figure of Eve with an apple—a clear reference to Mankiewicz's *All About Eve*, in which Bette Davis, Anne Baxter and a very young Marilyn Monroe are at daggers drawn. In some cases, the figures are replaced by silhouettes. One is reminded of the very famous Fred Astaire solo in which he dances with shadows. Finally there is the series of *Frames*, which seem identical but are each slightly different (due to tiny shifts and displacements). Here again, the title is no accident, referring as it does to film frames, whose unbroken succession makes it possible for the individual poses of photography to unfurl in a dance.

Untitled, 1997
Pencil and ink on paper, 24 x 33 cm

Untitled, 1997
Pencil and ink on paper, 24 x 33 cm

Works

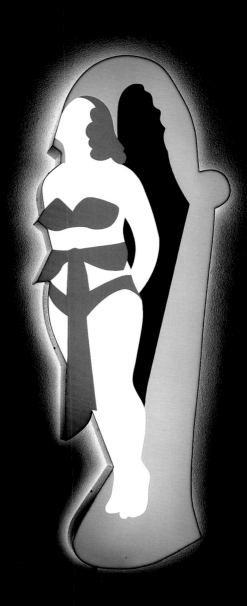

Eclipse, 1997

Perspex and neon
120 × 45 × 12 cm

Cuspide, 1997
Perspex and neon
140 × 59 × 12 cm

Stars and Bars, 1997
Perspex and neon
430 × 180 × 12 cm (overall)

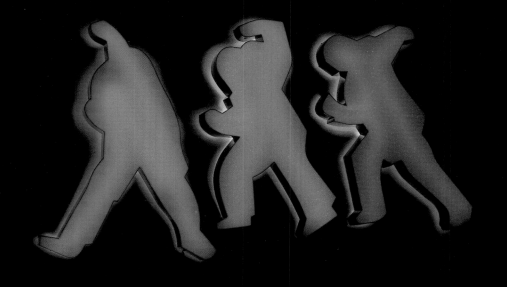

D3 Vita, 1997
Perspex and neon
300 × 150 × 12 cm (overall)

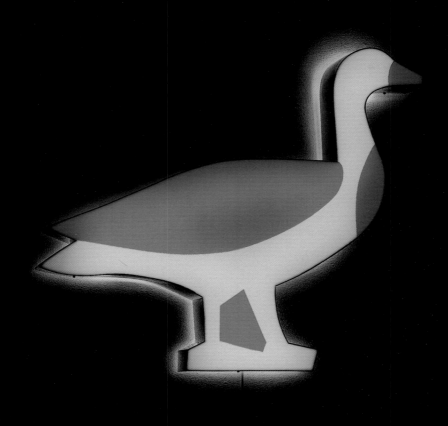

Oca di Meidum, 1997
Perspex and neon
62 × 73 × 10 cm

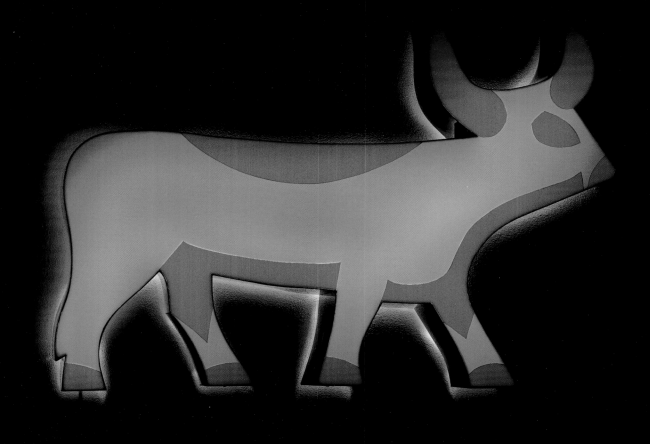

Athor, 1997
Perspex and neon
65 × 70 × 10 cm

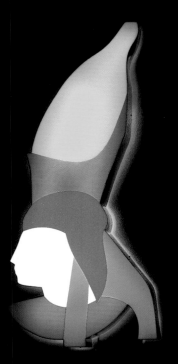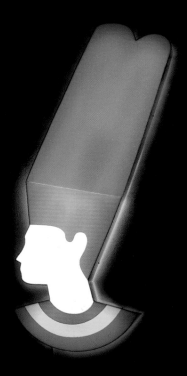

Ramses I, Ramses IV, and Amenofi I, 1997
Perspex and neon
250 × 120 × 12 cm (overall)

Ramses I, 1997
Perspex and neon
115 × 50 × 12 cm

W'illy, 1997
Perspex and neon
137 × 95 × 12 cm

Max.883, 1997
Perspex and neon
120 × 97 × 12 cm

Omar, 1997
Perspex and neon
116 × 97 × 12 cm

Edo, 1997
Perspex and neon
120 × 100 × 12 cm

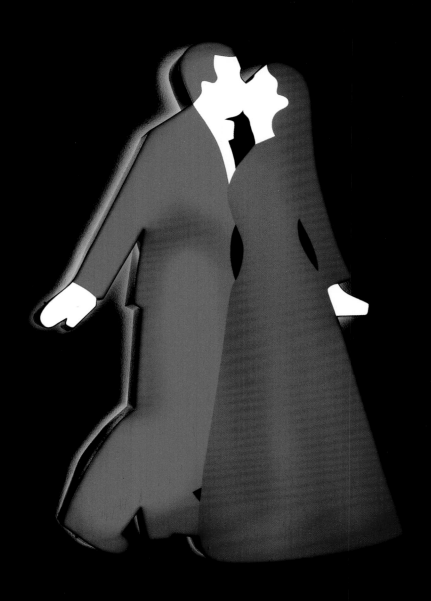

Frames, 1997
Perspex and neon
$100 \times 60 \times 12$ cm

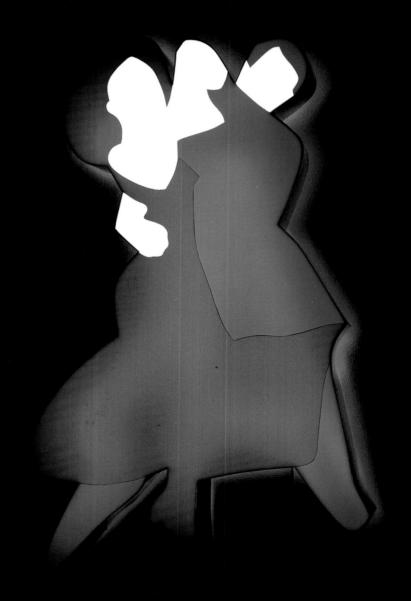

Surface, 1997
Perspex and neon
110 × 55 × 12 cm

Blues, 1997
Perspex and neon
88 × 53 × 12 cm

Musical, 1997
Perspex and neon
100 × 55 × 12 cm

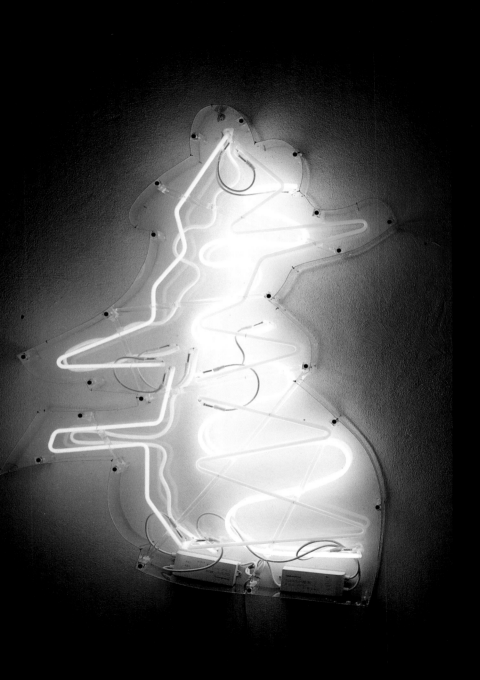

Inner City Lights, 1997
Perspex and neon
130 × 110 × 12 cm

Ballet Blanc, 1997
Perspex and neon
110 × 90 × 10 cm

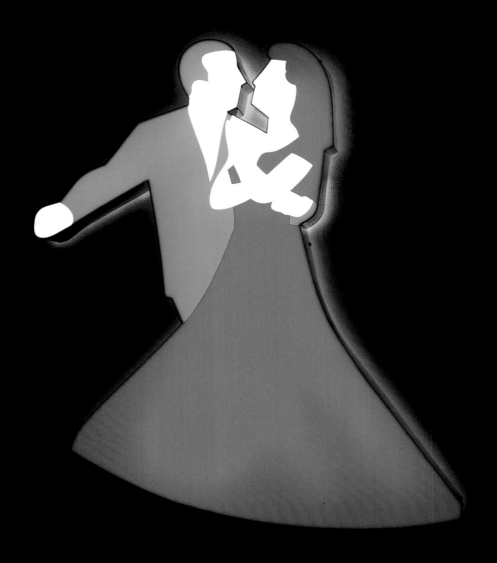

2000 Light Years from Home, 1997
Perspex and neon
$110 \times 75 \times 12$ cm

Pas de Deux, 1997
Perspex and neon
125 × 120 × 12 cm

Fruits, 1997
Perspex and neon
110 × 75 × 10 cm

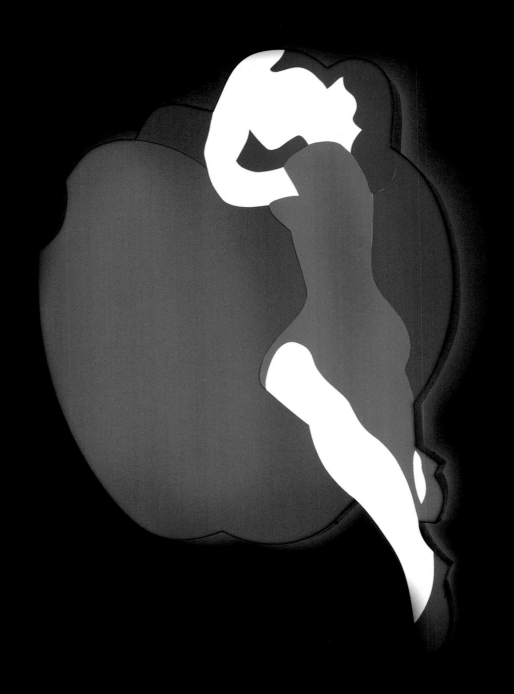

Ode, 1997
Perspex and neon
130 × 70 × 12 cm

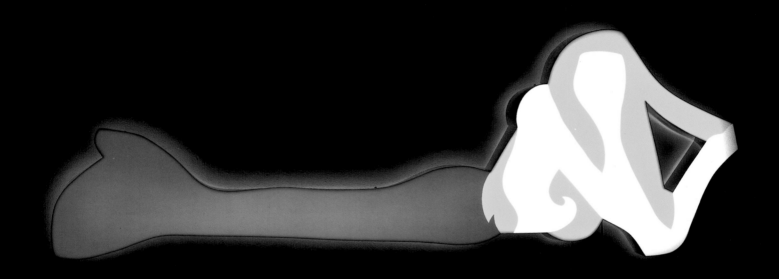

Sirenetta, 1997
Perspex and neon
50 × 145 × 10 cm

Kaos Time, 1997
Perspex and neon
125 × 75 × 10 cm

Quiz Show, 1997
Perspex, neon and sheet metal
420 × 80 × 40 cm

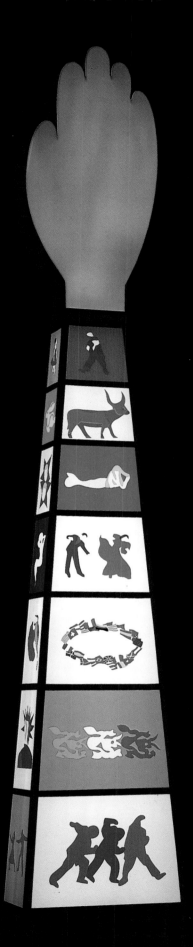

Deep Blue, 1996

Perspex, neon and sheet metal
285 × 130 × 50 cm

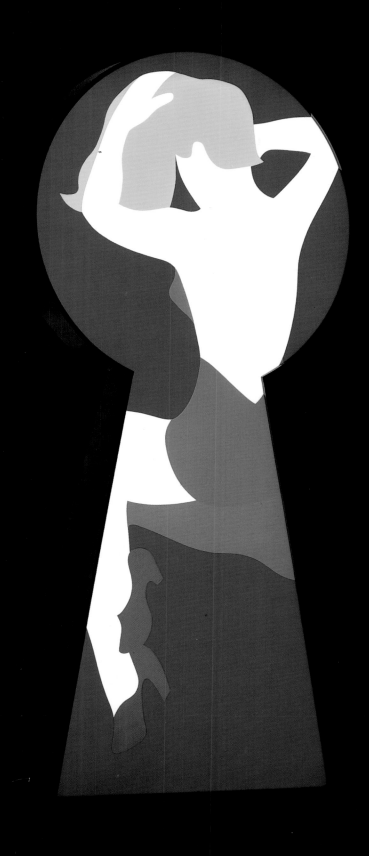

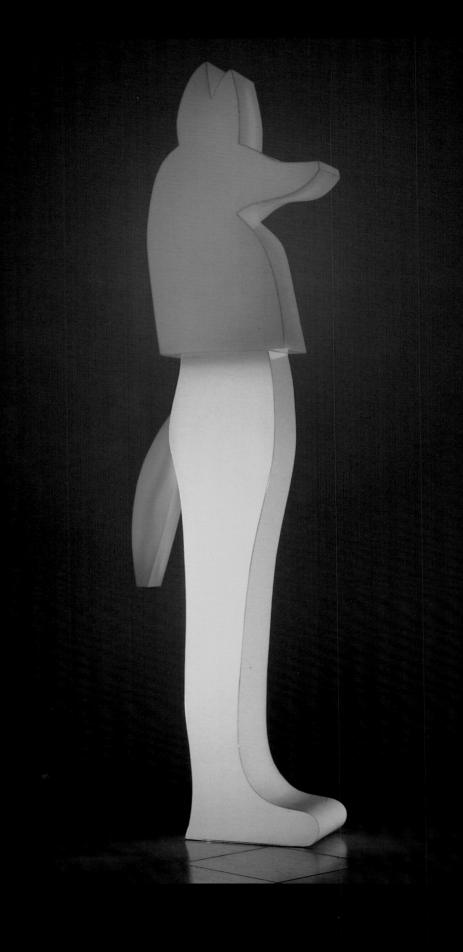

Anubis, 1997
Perspex, neon and sheet metal
265 × 70 × 23 cm

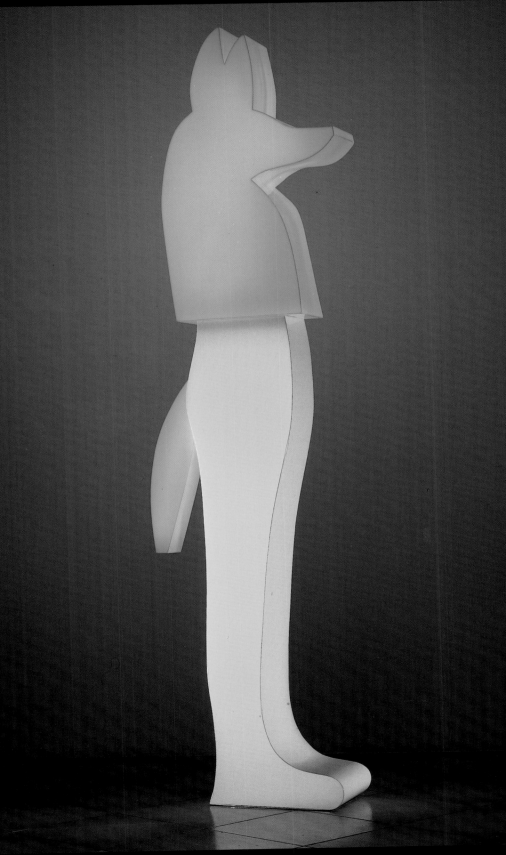

Nefertari, 1995
Perspex, neon and sheet metal
250 × 100 × 18 cm

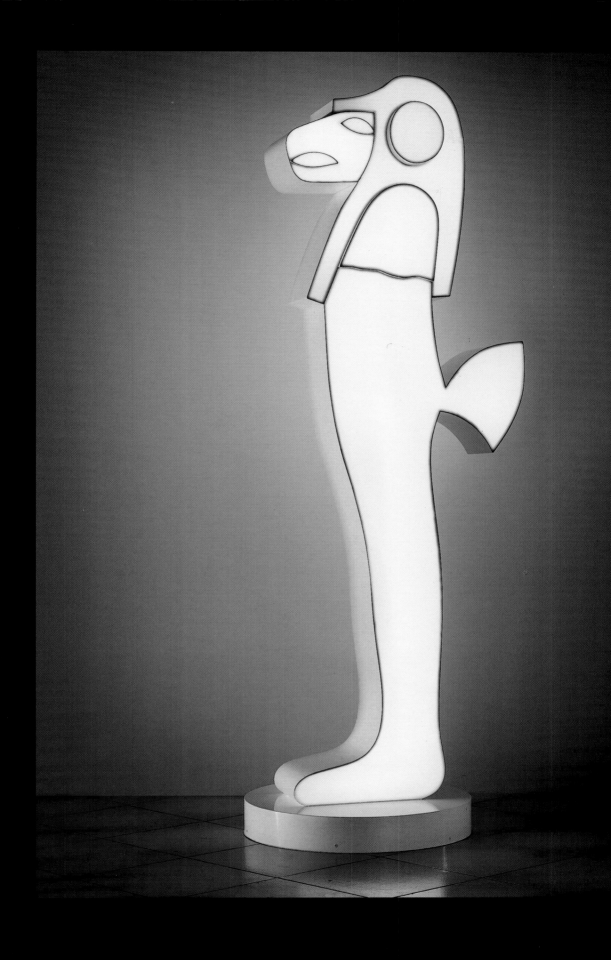

Rafiki, 1997
Perspex, neon and sheet metal
255 × 68 × 25 cm

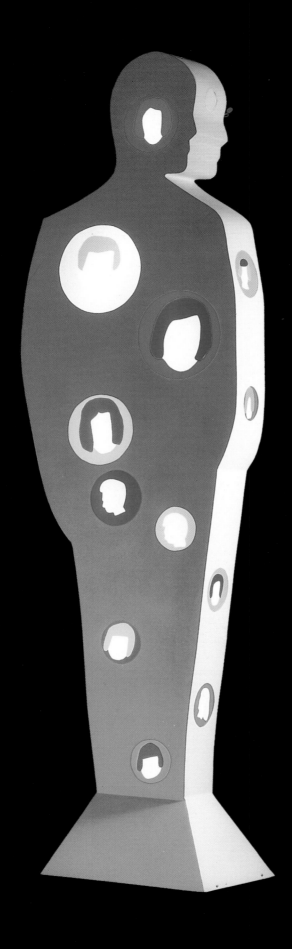

Klatu, 1995
Perspex, neon and sheet metal
255 × 70 × 20 cm

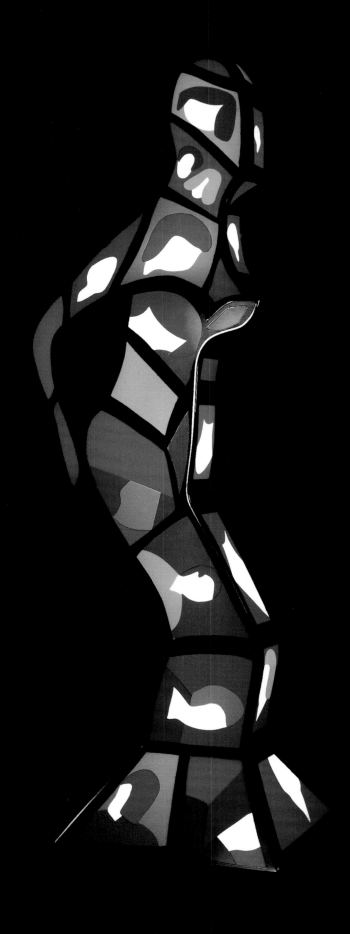

Video Follia, 1995
Perspex, neon and sheet metal
260 × 90 × 25 cm

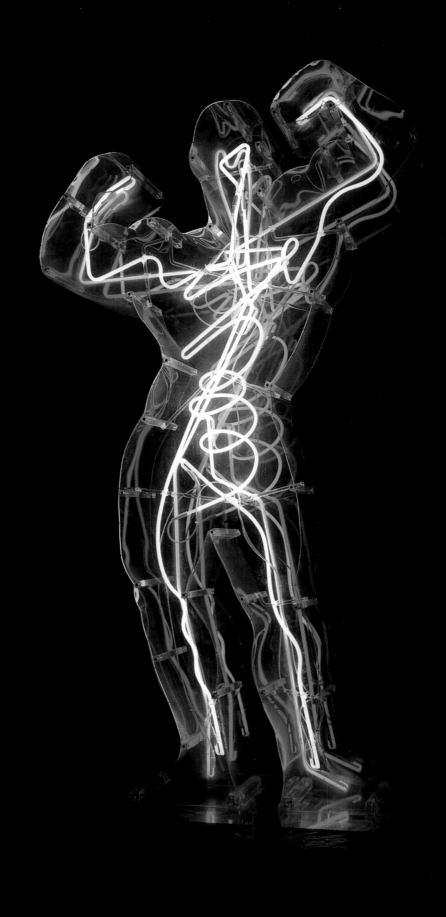

Clitunno, 1995
Perspex and neon
290 × 155 × 40 cm

Betsabea, 1995
Perspex and neon
245 × 200 × 35 cm

Untitled, 1997
Pencil and ink on paper, 24 x 33 cm

Appendices

Biography

Born in Dorno (Pavia) in 1955, Marco Lodola studied at the Florence and Milan Academies of Fine Arts. In the early eighties he was one of the artists who founded the "Nuovo Futurismo" movement, the theoretical spokesman of which was the critic Renato Barilli.

As a member of Nuovo Futurismo he exhibited in such major Italian and European cities as Rome, Florence, Bologna, Lyons, Vienna, Madrid and Amsterdam.

In 1994 he was invited by the Government of the Republic of China to hold an exhibition in the ex-Archives of the Imperial City of Beijing.

Marco Lodola has also participated at exhibitions promoted by companies such as Swatch, Coca Cola, Vini Ferrari and Snoopy. In 1996 he began a series of exhibitions in America, showing his work in Miami, Boca-Raton and the Marisa del Re Gallery, New York.

He participated in the 12th Rome Quadriennale and the 6th Montecarlo Sculpture Biennial. His works have also enjoyed great success in the world of publishing: since making the acquaintance of the writer Marco Lodoli he has designed the covers of his most recent novels. One of Lodola's works was also chosen to be on the cover of a volume of writings by the seventeenth century Japanese writer Ihara Saukaku, published by Frassinelli in its "I Classici" series (series editor: Aldo Busi).

Exhibitions

One Man
1985
Galleria La Polena, Genoa

1987
Galleria Il Capricorno, Venice
Galleria Fac-simile, Milan

1988
Galleria Ponte Pietra, Verona
Studio Cavalieri, Bologna

1989
Galleria Il Nome, Vigevano (Pavia)
Galleria VSV, Turin

1990
Galleria La Nuova Pesa, Rome
Studio Raffaelli, Trent

1991
Centro Steccata 2, Milan

1992
Studio d'Arte Duomo, Terni

1993
"Minestrone," Galleria La Nuova Pesa,
Rome
Galleria Mariottini, Arezzo
"Paint it black," EOS Arte Contemporanea,
Milan
Aula Magna, Università degli Studi,
Genoa
Istituto Italiano di Cultura, London

1994
Galleria Miralli, Viterbo
Palazzo Guasco, Alessandria
Studio Marconi, Milan

Galleria Peola, Turin
Wan-Fung Archives of the Forbidden City,
Beijing

1995
Galleria Galliata, Piacenza
Centro La Steccata, Parma

1996
"Pavese soup," Margaret Lipworth Arts,
Boca Raton
"Lodola 1976–96," Palazzo Farnese, Ortona
(Chieti)
"Video Follies," Palazzo Bricherasio, Turin
"Movie Stills," Marisa Del Re Gallery,
New York
"Blues oltremare," Galleria Cesarea, Genoa
"Smalto sul nulla," Galleria Giulia, Rome

1997
Galleria Ronchini, Terni
"Tinte forti," Galleria Galliata, Piacenza
"Mery en mut," Galleria Calvasina, Milan
"Trademark," Galleria Spazia, Bologna
"Racconti variopinti," Galleria Estense,
Ferrara
Galleria Menzani, Alassio (Savona)
"Musical-mente," Galleria Dialoghi, Biella
"Arte Fiera," Galleria Menhir, Barcelona
"Home Gallery," Pietrogrande Marchi,
Florence
Festival delle Nazioni, Città di Castello
(Perugia)
"Frames," Palazzo Civico, Galleria Menhir,
Sarzana (Spezia)
"Frames," Teatro Accademico, Casa del
Giorgione, Castelfranco Veneto
"Frames," Sala Bardolini, Palazzo Ducale,
Sassuolo (Modena)
"Self-Portraits," Galleria Bagnai, Siena

1998

"Inner City Lights," Marisa Del Re, New York

"Le ballet plastique," Galerie Pascal Lansberg, Paris

"Surface," Ambrosino Gallery, Miami

"Works on Paper," Margaret Lipworth Gallery, Boca Raton

"Video-Folies," Istituto Italiano di Cultura, Paris

Group
1983

"Home Sweet Home," Galleria Diagramma, Milan

1984

"New look in the Bodo's house," Galleria Diagramma, Milan

"Nuovo Futurismo," Galleria Pellegrino, Bologna

"Hangar tempo di guerra tempo di pace," Galleria Diagramma, Milan

"Nuovo Futurismo," Galerie Grita Insam, Vienna

"Cravatta al museo," Palazzo Inghirami, Milan

"Nuovo Futurismo," Art Fair, Basel

1985

"Nuovo Futurismo," Groningen Museum, Groningen

"Neofuturpanth," Galleria Pantha Arte, Como

"Saluti dall'Italia," Luisa Showroom, Florence

"Vetrine ad arte," Genoa

"Anniottanta," Castel Sismondo, Rimini

"A est e a ovest del crepuscolo," former Convento di S. Pietro, Asolo

"Modi e maniere della nuova esteticità," Galleria VSV, Turin

1986

"Nuovo Futurismo," Galerie Severine Teucher, Zurich

"Nuovo Futurismo," Rotonda della Besana, Milan

"Effetto Placebo," ICAF/Art Fair, London

"Ssswatchgalà," Superstudio, Milan

"Dopo il concettuale," Museo delle Albere, Trent

"Time out," Bari

1987

"Effetto Placebo," Galleria Murnik, Milan

"Step of an artist," Bossi Showroom, New York

"Effetto Placebo," Galleria Siquer, Madrid

"Nuovo Futurismo," Kaess-Wess Gallery, Stockholm

"Sagome e Tracce," Carpi (Modena)

"La pittura verso gli anni Ottanta," Civica Galleria, Gallarate (Varese)

"Nuovo Futurismo," Associazione Esca, Nîmes

"Equinozio d'autunno," Castello di Rivara, Turin

"Nouveaux futuristes," Centre d'Arts Plastiques Saint-Fons, Lyons

"La caverna elettronica, la nuova immagine," Civico Museo, Torre Pellice

"Nuovo Futurismo," Studio Raffaelli, Trent

1988

"Araldica, Studio Cavalieri," Bologna

"Geometrie Dionisiache," Rotonda della Besana, Milan

"Araldica," Casa Veneta, Muggia (Trieste)

"Microdrammi," Galleria Fac-simile, Milan

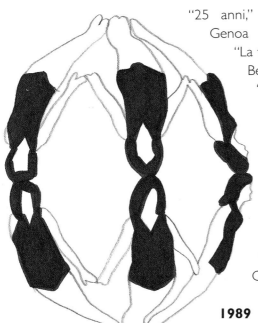

"25 anni," Galleria La Polena, Genoa

"La terza dimensione," San Benedetto Po (Mantua)

"Punto Uno," Studio Marconi, Milan

"Nuove acquisizioni," Galleria Nazionale d'Arte Moderna, Bologna

"Araldica," Concordia sulla Secchia (Modena)

"Video lento," Studio Casoli, Milan

1989

"Punto Uno," Mara Coccia, Rome

"Punto Uno," Nicola Verlato, Bologna

"Mediterraneo," Art Fair, Bari

"Punto Uno," Galleria La Polena, Genoa

"Punto Uno," La Nuova Bussola, Turin

"Singolare/Plurale," Galleria Diagramma, Milan

"Nuovo Futurismo," Istituto Italiano di Cultura, Madrid

"Nuovo Futurismo," Art Fair, Basel

"Nuovo Futurismo," Galerie Am Rindermarkt 26, Zurich

"Nuovo Futurismo," La Macchina dell'Arte, Biella

"VSV 88–89," Galleria VSV, Turin

"Art Junction," Nice

"XXLX Premio Città di Suzzara," Galleria Civica, Suzzara (Mantua)

"Nuovo Futurismo," Studio Frigieri, Carpi (Modena)

"L'immagine e il concetto," Palazzo della Porta, Gubbio (Perugia)

1990

"Nuevo Futurismo," Istituto Italiano di Cultura, Palma di Majorca

"Nuovo Futurismo," Galleria Triagono, Nola (Naples)

"Nuovo Futurismo," Galleria Murnik, Milan

"La più bella galleria d'Italia," Studio Frigieri, Florence

"Artefax," Galleria Nazionale d'Arte Moderna, Bologna

"Innocente, Plumcake, Abate, Lodola," Studio Frigieri, Carpi (Modena)

"Openings," Primo Piano Gallery, Milan

1991

"Nuovo Futurismo," Palazzo Guasco, Alessandria

"Nuovo Futurismo," Galleria Rino Costa, Casale Monferrato (Alessandria)

"Abate, Lodola, Innocente, Plumcake," Centro La Steccata, Parma

"Effetto Placebo 91," Galleria Murnik, Castel S. Pietro (Bologna)

"50 volte VSV," Galleria VSV, Turin

"Internazionale d'Arte," Galleria Fac-simile, Milan

"Operazione S. Giustino," Via Solferino, Milan

"La ragione trasparente," EOS Arte Contemporanea, Milan

Studio Frigieri, Castello la Volpaia, Florence

"Le ragioni dei cuore," Galleria Container, Florence

Galleria G. Mariottini, Arezzo

1992

"Nuovo Futurismo," Galleria Sorrenti, Novara

"Un inventaire," Esca Gallery, Nîmes

"La ragione trasparente 2," EOS Arte Contemporanea, Madonna di Campiglio (Trent)

"Nuovo Futurismo," Galleria Fontanella Borghese, Rome

"Arte Fiera Bologna," Galleria Steccata 2, Milan

"La più bella galleria d'Italia," La Nuova Pesa, Florence

"Cocart," Galleria Bianca Pilat, Milan-Verona-Mantua-Bari

"Il mondo di Snoopy," Spazio Flaminio, Rome-Milan-Venice

"Nuove acquisizioni," Bolzano

1993

"Il consumo disegnato, il disegno consumato," Palazzo delle Esposizioni, Rome

"Découvertes," Grand Palais, Paris

"New Futurism," Galleria T. Levi, Hamburg

"Nuovo Futurismo," Galleria La Pesa, Monza (Milan)

"Artisti D.O.C.," Spazio Ferrari, Trent

"Cocart," Spazio Flaminio, Rome

"A scatola chiusa," Galleria Via Farini, Milan

"Il mondo di Snoopy," Rotonda della Besana, Milan

"Esagono," Studio Frigieri, Rubiera (Reggio Emilia)

"Arte Novanta," Comune di Ravarino (Modena)

"Patchworking," Associazione Pratello, Bologna

"A onor del falso," Palazzo delle Esposizioni, Rome

"La ragione trasparente 3," Galleria EOS, Milan

"Art is life," Museo dell'automobile, Turin; Grand Museum-PMMK, Ostende; Sotheby's, Palazzo Broggi, Milan

"Art & Tabac," Spazio Flaminio, Rome

"Scarperentola," Idea Books, Milan

"Le materie inventate," Museo d'Arte Mo-

derna, Gazoldo degli Ippoliti (Mantua)

"Rentrée," Premio Marche 93, Ancona

"Art & Tabac," Palazzo Ruspoli, Rome

"Rosa d'inverno," Galleria EOS, Milan

"Un Milion," Galleria Bianca Pilat, Milan

1994

"Misure uniche," Galleria Il Politico, Rome; Galleria Bianca Pilat, Milan; University of Ancona

"Scarperentola," Lignano Sabbiadoro (Udine)

"Arte in maschera," Borgosesia (Novara)

"Jambo Jambo," Galleria Comunale d'Arte, Cesena (Forlì)

"Legnaghi, Ronconi, Lodola," Galleria Cinquetti, Verona

"Le tavole della legge," Galleria Catelani, Castello della Volpaia (Florence)

"Consigli di fabbrica," Galleria Comunale, Spoleto; Galleria La Nuova Pesa, Rome; Galleria Margiacchi, Arezzo

"Protagonista il mare," Galleria La Bussola, Turin

"Cinderella's Revenge," Cristinrose Gallery, New York

Bazar Atelier Mendini, Milan

"Nuovo Futurismo," Museo d'Arte Contemporanea, Rovereto; Loggia Balestrieri, S. Marino

"Arte for Eso," Fondazione Oncologica, Palazzo della Triennale, Milan

"Emergenze planetarie," Galleria Fontanella Borghese, Rome; Galleria La Giarina, Verona

"El magico mundo de Mickey Mouse," Palazzo Conde Duque, Madrid

"Multipli d'autore," Galleria Estense, Ferrara

1995

"Lùcida, Galleria San Rocco," Colorno (Parma)

"Cinderella's Revenge," Smith's Gallery-Covent Gallery, London; Jeddah Exhibition Center, Saudi Arabia; Lane Crawford, Hong Kong-Singapore; Passage de Retz Marais, Paris

"Yet-Yet-Yet–I legni di Pirondini," Galleria Bianca Pilat, Milan

"Giovane Arte Contemporanea," Castello di Sartirana (Pavia)

"Marinetti e il movimento Futurista," Palazzo Guasco, Alessandria

"Quando l'oro parla," Galleria Fallani, Florence

"Gioielli d'autore," Antwerp

"Acque d'autore," Rome; Galleria Fac-simile, Milan; Bologna

"Marilyn Monroe," Palazzo delle Civiltà, Rome

"Group show," Margaret Lipworth, Miami

"Un segno per il Sarno," Galleria Comunale d'Arte Moderna, Scafati (Salerno)

"Premio Vasto–Dall'Arte Povera al Postmoderno," Istituto Palazzi, Vasto (Chieti)

"Nel segno dell'angelo," Galleria Bianca Pilat, Milan

"Scarperentola," Galleria Niccoli, Parma

"Art Fair," Margaret Lipworth, Miami

1996

"European Design–Design as Identity," Louisiana Museum, Humlebaek (Denmark)

"Made in Art," Galleria Terzo Millennio, Milan

"Marilyn–Un mito," Lingotto, Turin

XIIth Quadriennale, Palazzo delle Esposizioni, Rome

"Ten Little Indians," Boca Raton Florida

"L'impero dei sensi," Il Triangolo, Cremona

"Riparte," Galleria Cesarea, Ripa Residence, Rome

"Sign of an angel," Pilat Gallery, Chicago

"Mitomodernismo," Galleria Galliata, Piacenza, curated by S. Zecchi

Premio "Do Forni," Venice

"Stellina di Natale," Graziella Lombardi, Naples

1997

"Design as Identity," Museum of Decorative Arts, Ghent (Belgium)

"Flowers–Un fiore per la vita," Palazzo Sala Lancisi, Rome

"Madrenatura," Palazzo dei Martinitt, Milan

"Universarte," S. Giovanni in Monte, Bologna, curated by Vittoria Coen

VIth Sculpture Biennial, Monte Carlo

"Va' pensiero–Arte italiana," Promotrice delle Belle Arti, Turin, curated by E. Di Mauro

"Unimplosive Art," Le Zitelle, Venice

Galleria Bagnai, F.I.A.C., Paris

Galleria Bagnai, Art Fair, Ghent (Belgium)

"Dal mito alla storia," Galleria Galliata, Alassio (Savona)

"Traguardo," Galleria Colombo, Milan

"Ritorno al mare," Palazzo Pascali, Polignano al Mare, Bari

"Superficies," The Gallery, Mexico City

"Sculture a Palazzo Zambeccari," Galleria Spazia, Bologna

"La terra trema," Galleria il Milione, Milan

"Novelle di un viaggiatore stanco," Galleria Artistudio, Milan

"Europa-USA," Palazzo Osterio Magno, Cefalù

1998

"Arte Fiera," Ambrosino Gallery

"Due o tre cose che sò di Loro," Padiglione di Arte Contemporanea, Milan

"Mito Ferrari," Museo di San Marino, San Marino

Bibliography

1983

E. Muritti, "Vado ad abitare a Babilonia," in *Il Giornale Nuovo*, 13 October

M. Angelus, "Casa dolce casa," in *Viva Milano*, no. 12, November

M. Castel, "Hanno messo nel sacco i graffiti anni Ottanta," in *La Repubblica*, 13 November

E. Cirone, "Bello stabile dal mondo," in *Il Buongiorno*, December

L. Inga Pin, "La trasgressione colta," in *S & M*, no. 1, December

L. Parmesani, "Home Sweet Home," in *Flash Art*, December

E. Muritti, "Quanto è caotico quello spettacolo," in *Il Giornale Nuovo*, 13 December

1984

G. Verzotti, "Un nuovo continente ironicamente cinico," in *Segno*, no. 35, February

L. Parmesani, "Nuovo Futurismo," in *Flash Art*, March–April

R. Barilli, "L'ornamento non è più un delitto," in *L'Espresso*, no. 13, April

D. Facchinato, A. Ruggeri, "Arte di Frontiera," in *Lei*, May

B. Gerosa, "Nuovo Look, Nuovo futurismo," in *Domus*, June

R. Schiess, "Es gibt eine uferlose Masse bewältigen," in *Nordschweiz*, 15 June

R. Barilli, "I nuovi futuristi," in *L'Espresso*, 1 July

R. Rozon, "Les Remous de la Foire de Bâle," in *La Vie des Arts*, Montreal, September

R. Simons, "Majesteus Milaan," in *Avenue*, no. 19, September

L. Somaini, "Nel nome del Futurismo ecco l'arte divertimento," in *La Repubblica*, 2 October

M. Kaufmann, "Il Nuovo Futurismo espone da Inga-Pin," in *Viva Milano*, 11 October

P.F. Damiani, "Nuovi futuristi: ecco il mondo degli oggetti," in *La Provincia Pavese*, 17 October

E. Muritti, "I nuovi futuristi siamo noi," in *Il Giornale Nuovo*, 30 October

C. Castellani, "Nuovi futuristi: l'industria è il nostro mondo," in *Annabella*, no. 46, November

E. Cirone, "Nell'hangar c'è il Nuovo Futurismo," in *Il Buongiorno*, November

A. Monteil, "Neue Wellen Sanfter Phantastik," in *Basler Zeitung*, 15 November

J. Tahor, "Leichtfrivole Kunstwerke mit banalen Späßen," in *Kurier*, 14 December

AA., "Ein neues la zur Vermarktung," in *Salzburger Tagblatt*, 17 December

K. Sottrifer, "Ein Erweitertes Zeitgefühl," in *Die Presse*, 17 December

M. Buchshaunt, "Künstlergruppen werden vorgestellt," in *Wiener Zeitung*, 20 December

H.G. Haberl, "Rosinen in Hirm," in *Kleine Zeitung*, 20 December

O. Wiesflecker, "Grenzüberschreitende," in *Volksstimme*, 28 December

E. Melchart, "Plastikkunst für Plastikwelt," in *Neu Kronen Zeitung*, 29 December

Catalogo a fumetti, edited by L. Inga Pin, Milan

Vincitorio, "Nuovo Futurismo, la parte dell'occhio," in *L'Espresso*

1985

R. Bonfiglioli, "Chi sale e chi scende," in *Per lui*, January

B. Maggiori, "I giovani produttori europei," in *Domus*, January

M.G. Torri, "Plumcake & C.," in *Frigidaire*, January

A. Vettese, "Hangar," in *Flash Gallerie*, January
R. Barilli, F. Haks, L. Inga Pin, *Nuovo Futurismo*, exhibition catalogue, Groningen Museum, Groningen
G. Magnani, "Tempo di guerra, tempo di pace," in *Juliet*, February
Niederma, "Nuovo Futurismo past her best in de etalage van de Bijenkorf," in *Nieuwsblad van ten Noorden*, Groningen, March
E. Cirone, "Nuovo Futurismo," in *Café Crème*, March–April
M.G. Torri, "Hangar: arte di guerra, arte di pace," in *Segno*, April
G. Verzotti, "New Futurism," in *Flash Art International*, April–May
E. Cirone, "Una polena made in Italy," in *Il Buongiorno*, May
M.L. Frisa, "Nuovo futurismo," in *Saluti dall'Italia*, exhibition catalogue, Luisa Showroom, Florence
Beringneli, "Vecchie cose di nuovi futurismi," in *Il Lavoro*, 27 May
E. Cirone, "Made in Italy," in *Segno*, June
D. Fedi, "È di moda la cultura," in *100 Cose*, June
L. Parmesani, "Nouveau Futurisme," in *L'Art vivant*, June
R. Daolio, "Decorazione, pittura veloce, spirito ludico," in *Anniottanta*, exhibition catalogue, Castel Sigismondo, Rimini
"L'avanguardia in mostra e in moda," in *Donna*, September
M.G. Torri, "A est e a ovest del crepuscolo," introduction to exhibition catalogue, former Convento di S. Pietro, Asolo, September
E. Muritti, "Dal bell'oggetto all'androide," in *Rassegna artistica-culturale*, September–October
E. Cirone, "Intervista a Luciano Inga Pin," in *Over*, December

Reitsma, "Het aankoopbeleid van Frans Haks: we doen nooit de anderen al doen," in *Vrij Nederland*, December
S. Sereni, "E l'artista torna allo studio," in *Panorama Mese*, December
M.G. Torri, "Rimini and Rimini," in *Flash Art*, December 1985–January 1986
M.G. Torri, "A est e a ovest del crepuscolo, le ragioni di una mostra," in *Flash Art*, December 1985–January 1986

1986
R. Barilli, "Futurismo prossimo venturo," in *L'Espresso*, 28 January
G. Frediani, "I nuovi futuristi," in *Lei*, February
L. Vergine, "I nuovi pittori," in *Panorama*, 16 February
R. Daolio, in *Reporter*, 21 February
Forum, catalogue of the Zurich International Art Fair, 20–24 February
M.G. Torri, "Marco Lodola. Arte e Religione," in *Frigidaire*, March
R. Pasini, "Dalla Pop al Postmoderno," in *Questarte*, March
L. Caramel, "Tutti al Forum con allegria," in *Il Giornale Nuovo*, 2 March
G.L. Paracchini, "Besanaottanta," in *Corriere della Sera*, 6 March
G. Ballabio, "Nuovi e Post alla Besana," in *ViviMilan*, 6 March
N. Aspesi, in *La Repubblica*, 8 March
A. Vettese, "Tra nuovo e post il debutto di Caroli-Barilli," in *Il Sole 24 Ore*, 10 March
R. Barilli, "Se il petrolio cala scatta l'avanguardia," in *Corriere della Sera*, 11 March
E. Cirone, "Nuovo Futurismo e Postastrazione," in *Gruppo Reporter*, 11 March
R. Pasini, "I terribili nipotini di Balla," in *Il Resto del Carlino*, 15 March
R. Bossaglia, "Tutti i nipoti di Balla," in *Cor-*

riere della Sera, 15 March

L. Bortolon, "Su il sipario è di scena il presente," in *Grazia*, 16 March

G. Mascherpa, "Besanaottanta: scampoli di vera pittura nello stanco degli in 'ISMI,'" in *Avvenire*, 21 March

U. Lo Russo, "Neofuturisti e postastratti," in *La Provincia*, 21 March

N. Pallini, "Futurismo e Astrazione," in *Gioia*, 21 March

R. Barilli, "I molti sentieri del bosco astratto," in *Corriere della Sera*, 22 March

L. Caramel, "I trentenni si divertono," in *Il Giornale Nuovo*, 23 March

F.B. Negri, "Besanottanta. Polemica," in *La Prealpina*, 27 March

D. Plescan, "Nuovo Futurismo," in *Rassegna clinico-scientifica*, March–April

R. Barilli, *Besanaottanta. Nuovo Futurismo*, exhibition catalogue, Rotonda della Besana, Milan, March–April

E. Di Mauro, "Nuovo Futurismo e Postastrazione," in *Segno*, April

Perry, "Besanaottanta," in *S.M.*, April

G. Seveso, "Besanaottanta. Come fabbricare le mode," in *Artecultura*, April

"Neofuturisti in forma sulla cresta dell'onda," in *Arte*, April

L. Maggi, "Besanaottanta," in *Vogue Italia*, 1 April

P.F. Damiani, "Ironia e suggestioni dei nuovi futuristi," in *La Provincia Pavese*, 2 April

E. Muritti, "Dall'oggetto all'androide," in *Rassegna artistica-culturale*, no. 5

L. Somaini, "Ecco gli Yuppies dell'Arte, la loro Mecca è sui Navigli," in *La Repubblica*, 5 April

A. Giacobino, "Rotonda della Besana ed è subito polemica per due mostre d'arte," in *La Provincia di Cremona*, 8 April

L. Tallarico, "Futurismo Boom," in *Il Secolo d'Italia*, 9 April

J. Jennaco, "Nuovo futurismo e Postastrazione," in *Spazio*, 17 April

A.C. Quintavalle, "Hanno un futuro i Nuovi Futuristi?," in *Panorama*, 27 April

G.M. Accame, "Postastrazione e neofuturismo alla Besana," in *Paese Sera*, 28 April

"Memphis alla Pantha Arte," in *Domina*, April–May

G. Verzotti, "I nuovi futuristi," in *Flash Art*, April–May

"Besanaottanta," in *Interni*, May

M.G. Torri, "I nuovi futuristi," in *Alfabeta*, May

E. Pontiggia, "Anniottanta ritorno alla pittura," in *Il Giornale Nuovo*, May

G. Massimini, "Nuovo Futurismo," in *Punto d'incontro Artitalia*, May

G. Frediani, "L'Arte giovane da nord a sud," in *Lei*, May

M.G. Torri, "Ciò che i nuovi futuristi non sono," in *Alfabeta*, June

O. Alfonso, L. Spadano, "Panorama delle tendenze in Italia una rincorsa all'esserci," in *Segno*, June

G. Harari, "Garboclima," in *Rockstar*, July

R. Barilli, "A grandi passi verso gli anni '90," in *Corriere della Sera*, 2 July

R. Barilli, "All'aperto c'è aria di chiuso," in *L'Espresso*, 27 July

E. Caroli, "Minidizionario. Gli anni '80," in *Art Dossier*, July–August

F. Fedi, "Collettivi e Gruppi Artistici a Milano," in *Nuovo Fu-*

turismo, September

R. Barilli, "Se la prospettiva è troppo personale," in *Corriere della Sera,* 17 September

A.C. Quintavalle, "Arte come Gioco," in *Panorama,* 12 October

W. Rainer, *Sisyphos malt Bilder,* November

"Nuovo Futurismo," in *Archiv,* 13 November

W.A. Von Runge, *Kunst mit Frischegarantie,* November–December

R. Barilli, F. Caroli, P. Weiermair, *Aspekte der Italienischen Kunst,* exhibition catalogue

R. Barilli, F. Caroli, *1960–1985 Aspekte der Italienischen Kunst,* exhibition catalogue, Frankfurter Kunstverein, Frankfurt

L. Caramel, *Arte in Italia: gli anni 90. Dopo il Concettuale: Nuove Generazioni in Lombardia,* exhibition catalogue, Trent

A. Pansera, M. Vitta, *Guida all'arte contemporanea,* Milan

R. Tsushin, "All about Italy," in *New Futurism,* Tokyo

E. Di Mauro, "I nuovi futuristi," in *Art Line*

F. Abbate, "La persistenza del gioco," in *Nuovi Argomenti*

1987

R. Barilli, *La pittura verso gli anni '90,* exhibition catalogue, Gallarate

M.G. Torri, V. Erlindo, *Sagome e tracce,* exhibition catalogue, Comune di Capri

J. La Page, *Nouveaux Futuristes,* exhibition catalogue, Gallerie Esca, Nîmes

L. Somaini, "Effetto Placebo," in *La Repubblica,* 30 January

G. Vincenzo, "Nomi e Quotazioni," in *Per lui,* February

S. Tonchi, "Passo d'Artista," in *Westuff,* February

"Step of an Artist," in *Footwear News,* February

M.G. Torri, "Marco Lodola," in *Flash Art,* February

R. Barilli, *Effetto Placebo,* exhibition catalogue, March

A. Murgia, "Effetto Placebo," in *Il Giorno,* 3 March

L. Bortolon, "Effetto Placebo," in *Grazia,* 3 March

L. Cavadini, "Effetto Placebo," in *La Provincia,* 5 March

G. Collado, "Nuevas tendencias de l'arte italiana," in *Guida dell'olio,* Madrid, 6 March

G. Manfredini, "Passo d'Artista," in *L'Unità,* 8 March

"Por un Arte 'Light,'" in *El Pais,* Madrid, 13 March

M. Logrono, "Nuevos Futuristas," in *Diario 16,* Madrid, 14 March

A. Sala, "Effetto Placebo," in *Corriere della Sera,* 18 March

R. Imwinkelried, "Neue Futuristen," in *Panorama,* Stuttgart

R. Barilli, "Ornamento d'obbligo per un neomoderno," in *Corriere della Sera,* 12 April

E. Di Mauro, "L'arte tra Sagome e Tracce," in *L'Avanti,* 24 April

M. Meneguzzo, "Effetto Placebo," in *Segno,* May

G. Vincenzo, "Nuovi spazi, Nuove voci," in *Per lui,* May

N. Cantaroni, "Bruna Bossi. Farò le scarpe all'uomo," in *Amica,* 29 June

S. Rizzardi, "Sagome–Tracce," in *Flash Art,* May–June

M.G. Torri, E. Di Mauro, "Gentili e Sospiri, Sagome e Tracce," in *Frigidaire,* July

M.G. Torri, E. Di Mauro, "Arte e seduzione," in *Frigidaire,* July

E. Vincitorio, in *Tutto libri,* 25 July

O. Ronda Aprile, "L'ultimo stadio del Futu-

rismo," in *Il Piacere*, August

R. Barilli, "Il Grande Freddo," in *L'Espresso*, 30 August

A. Mistrangelo, in *Stampa Sera*, 1 September

A.M. Mazzarella, "Mecenate sarà lei," in *Gente Money*, September

"Tran Diep. Surenchere neo pathe," in *Liberation*, October

"Les Nouveaux Futuristes," in *Lyon Boche*, Octobre des arts, October

"Le vernissage des Nouveaux Futuristes," in *Lyon Matin*, October

B. Bost, "Les Nouveaux Futuristes," in *Le Monde*, October

N. Colin, "Récupération Abusive," in *Lyon Figaro*, October

"Moda inserto," in *Panorama*, October

"Les Nouveaux Futuristes," in *Lyon Figaro*, 30 October

R. Barilli, *Il ciclo del post-moderno*

E. Calvi, "Marco Lodola," in *City*, November

R. Barilli, O. Goni, *Lodola. Monografia*, November

L. Maggi, in *Casa Vogue*, December

G. Turroni, in *Viva Milano*, December

E. Di Mauro, *La Caverna elettronica*, exhibition catalogue, Torre

O. Calabrese, *L'età neobarocca*, Bari

E. Baj, *Impariamo la pittura*, Milan

1988

D. Eccher, "Vogliono far rinascere," in *L'Adige*, January

F. Degasperi, "Futurismo, no grazie," in *Alto Adige*, January

L. Serravalli, "New Futurism, i nipoti di Depero," in *Trento*, January

M. Sisto, "Un vecchio rocher," in *Eva*, January

E. Calvasina, "Marco Lodola," in *Juliet*, February–March

E. Di Mauro, in *Juliet*, February–March

F. Abbate, "Arte," in *Playboy*, March

M. Gandini, "Marco Lodola," in *Flash Art*, March–April

P. Peduzzi, "Geometrici ma dionisiaci," in *Il Giornale dell'Arte*, April

C. Caligaris, "Trasparenze," in *Per lui*, April

L. Vergine, *Geometrie Dionisiache*, Milan

L. Vergine, *L'arte in gioco*, Milan

G. Barigazzi, "Arte," in *Il Piacere*, May

P. Tedeschi, "Arte Giovane Milano," in *Vogue Italia*, May

T. Thorimbert, C. Nunez, M. Rotini, "Flower power," in *Rockstar*, May

P. Jori, "In Italia oggi l'arte giovane," in *Gran Bazaar*, May

S. Sereni, "Teorema d'artista," in *Epoca*, May

O. Calabrese, L. Pratesi, "Gioventù quotata," in *Panorama*, May

L. Cabutti, "Grandi mostre," in *Arte*, May

D. Auregli, "I nuovi araldici del 2000," in *L'Unità*, 8 May

B. Tomasi, "Oggi in Italia l'arte giovane," in *L'illustrazione Italiana*, May–June

F. Durante, "I dionisiaci," in *Il Mattino*, 7 June

M. Amari, "Galleria Fac-Simile," in *Gran Milan*, June

F. Dentice, "I non replicanti," in *L'Espresso*, June

M.G. Quaroni, "Italia giovane di scena a Milano," in *Marie Claire*, June

A. Antolini, "Dioniso messo in vetrina," in *Il Giornale*, June

R. Barilli, "Sostenere l'arte con un'abile promozione," in *Corriere della Sera*, June

J.R. Taylor, "New from Italy," in *The Time*, July

A. Murgia, "Arte giovane made in Italy," in *Il Giorno*, 29 July

A. Romeo, "C'è spazio a disposizione dei giovani pittori?," in *Il Moderno*, August

O.R. Aprile, "Poesia nel plexiglass," in *Uomo*

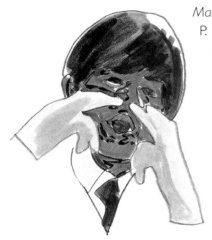

Manager, August

P. Restany, "Geometrie Dionisiache," in *Domus*, August

R. Pasini, "Arte," in *Alfabeta*, August

N. Maeyama, "Marco Lodola," in *Wind*, Tokyo, August

F.A. Miglietti, *Arte in Italia, 1960–1985*, September

"Chi sono i giovani artisti," in *Casa Viva*, September

E. Di Mauro, V. Erlindo, G. Pelizzola, *La Terza dimensione*, exhibition catalogue, September

G.P. Vincenzo, "Marco Lodola," in *Arte in Umbria*, September–October

C. Branzaglia, "La conciliazione dei contrari," in *Segno*, October

A. Clementi, "Marco il nuovo futurista," in *La Piazza*, October

R. Barilli, *Ordine e disordine*, exhibition catalogue, October

L. Cavallari, "E le linee fanno pop," in *Il Resto del Carlino*, 22 October

R. Vitali, "Marco Lodola," in *Mongolfiera*, November

S. Giacomoni, "Il bianco e il nero," in *L'Espresso*, November

1989

V. Coen, "Marco Lodola," in *Segno*, January

"Verona Arte Contemporanea," in *Egoista*, February

V. Cerabolini, "M. Lodola," in *Lei*, March

D.A. Peyranni, "Uno, due, tre Marco Lodola ci fa ballare," in *La Stampa*, March

"I plexiglass fiabeschi di Marco Lodola," in *La Stampa*, 3 March

R. Barilli, "La terza ondata appartiene alla mente," in *L'Espresso*, 9 April

R. Barilli, *Nuovo Futurismo*, exhibition catalogue, Madrid

"M. Lodola," in *La Provincia Pavese*, May

A Fiz, "Per i futuristi la provocazione è un business," in *Milano Finanza*, July

"Los nuevas futuristas," in *Epoca*, Madrid, July

R. Pinto, "Singolare Plurale," in *Flash Art*, July–August

D. van Burg, *Nuovo Futurismo*, exhibition catalogue, Zurich

C. Wolf, "Missionare des Gewöhnlichen," in *Tages Anzeiger*, Zurich, August

E. Di Mauro, *L'immagine e il concetto*, exhibition catalogue, Gubbio

Var. Authors, "Tutti i giovani al premio rinato," in *Il Sole 24 Ore*, 22 October

M. Conti, "Quando l'arte è di moda," in *La Stampa*, 27 October

M. Gardella, G. Pino, in *L'Uomo Vogue*, November

F. Mondello, "Nuovo Futurismo," in *Eco di Biella*, 3 November

B. Pozzato, "I nuovi futuristi," in *Eco di Biella*, 3 November

Arte Moderna, no. 25, Milan

L. Papa, "Il Nord," in *Arte fiera*

1990

E. Gandini, exhibition catalogue for the Nuova Pesa Gallery, Rome

F. Degasperi, exhibition catalogue for the Studio Raffaelli, Trent

La Galleria più bella d'Italia, exhibition catalogue, Fortezza da Basso, Florence

M. Lodola, *I fannulloni*, Milan (cover)

L. Serravalli, "Neofuturisti," in *Alto Adige*, 6 March

C. Cerritelli, *Artefax*, exhibition catalogue, Bologna

A. Boralevi, "Un artista a passo di danza," in *Gioia*, November

K. Iwakura, in *Gulliver*

S. Dell'Orso, "Gli artisti dell'anno," in *Arte*, December

M.D.C., "Quanti danzatori per Lodola," in *La Repubblica*
Arte Moderna, no. 26, Milan

1991

F. Francione, "M. Lodola, geometria quotidiana," in *Il cittadino di Lodi*

M. Senaldi, R. Barilli, *Nuovo Futurismo*, exhibition catalogue, Casale Monferrato

R. Barilli, Introduction to the exhibition catalogue, Palazzo Guasco, Alessandria

M. Senaldi, *Marco Lodola*, exhibition catalogue, Pavia

M. Genova, "Le danze trasparenti di Marco Lodola," in *Made in Biella*

G. Vallese, "Gli anni '80," in *Arte*

"A. Galletta, M. Lodola M. Lodoli," in *Il temporale*, Lugano

G. Ciavoliello, *Operazione S. Giustino*, Milan

E.P., "Un sorriso e uno schiaffo," in *Il Resto del Carlino*

M.L. Frisa, exhibition catalogue, Galleria Mariottini, Arezzo

C. Perella, "Nuovi Futuristi," in *Proposte*, 11 June

G. Odoni, "Capriccio milanese," in *Casa Vogue*, September

"S. Tonchi, A. Zordan, M. Lodola," in *L'Uomo Vogue*, September

P. Zambrano, "La regione trasparente," in *Corriere della Sera*, 10 September

G. Ciavoliello, in *Juliet*, December

1992

M. Lodoli, "Marco Lodola," in *Taxiart*

A. Bonito Oliva, J. Keller, *Cocart*, exhibition catalogue, Milan

"M. Lodola al nuovo centro," in *Arte*, Milan

P.F. Damiani, poster illustration for Unicef, May

A. Fiz, "Cocart," in *Italia Oggi*, 10 May

R. Bossaglia, "Cocart," in *Corriere della Sera*, 24 May

L. Bortolon, "Mille bollicine di Cocart," in *Grazia*, 31 May

E. Di Mauro, in *Juliet*, June

G. Mazzotti, "Coca Cola della ragione," in *La Gazzetta*, Mantua, 5 July

G. Mazzotti, "Furto alla mostra Cocart," in *La Gazzetta*, Mantua, 9 July

F. Pini, "Cocart," in *Sette*, (*Corriere della Sera* supplement), 12 July

Coppola, "Cocart," in *Gazzetta di Bari*, September

L. Papa, "Nuovo Futurismo alla galleria Sorrenti," in *Il Nord*, 1 October

Auction catalogue, Auction Phila, 16 November

M. De Candia, "Ecco i nuovi futuristi," in *La Repubblica*, 3 December

C. Strano, *Il mondo di Snoopy*, exhibition catalogue, Rome

S. Petricca, exhibition catalogue, Fontanella Borghese, Rome

R. Barilli, exhibition catalogue, Studio d'Arte, Terni

S. Grandi, *La moda nel II dopoguerra*, Bologna

1993

E. Grazioli, exhibi-

tion catalogue, Galleria Mariottini, Arezzo

R. Barilli, *Il consumo disegnato*, exhibition catalogue, Rome

R. Barilli, M. Lodola, in *L'Espresso*, January

"Il sigillo della qualità," in *Tavola*, January

R. Barilli, "Ballerine futuriste," in *L'Espresso*, 25 January

V. Apulco, "Lodola tra fantasia e progettazione," in *Il Messaggero*, 27 January

"Paint it black," in *Milano 90*, February

F. Francione, "Lodola 10 anni di neofuturista," in *La Provincia Pavese*, 4 February

"I ballerini di M. Lodola," in *La Repubblica*, 5 February

M. Garzonio, "Balletto in plexiglass," in *ViviMilano*, 10 February

G. Garlando, "M. Lodola ambiguità in plexiglass," in *Il Giorno*, 11 February

"M. Lodola," in *Il Manifesto*, 13 February

D. Facchinetti, "Marco Lodola," in *TV Sorrisi e Canzoni*, 14 February

"M. Lodola," in *TuttoMilano*, 18 February

E. Muritti, "Appuntamenti con la scultura," in *Il Giornale*, 18 February

S. Bonzi, "La danza per M. Lodola," in *Alba*, 19 February

M. Carboni, "I ritagli arerei di M. Lodola," in *La Repubblica*, 19 February

"La sua collezione di ballerine," in *L'Europeo*, 19 February

L. Mosconi, "Danze rituali in bianco e nero," in *La Provincia*, Como, 20 February

A. Fiz, "Ballando ballando," in *M.F.*, 20 February

M.V. Carloni, "Son tornato in me," in *Panorama*, 21 February

R. Dell'Acqua, "Movimenti vitali," in *Inchiostro*, March

"Tanto per giocare," in *Cosmopolitan*, March

F. Abbate, "M. Lodola," in *Playboy*, March

G. Cavallo, "Bianco, rosso e coke," in *Settimana TV e tempolibero*, 4 March

P. Ugolini, "M. Lodola," in *Flash Art*, April

A. Bevilacqua, "Bottiglie d'arte," in *Alto Adige*, 23 April

"Fantasia imbottigliata," in *Il Sole 24 Ore*, 24 April

"Artisti D.O.C.," in *L'Indipendente*, 25 April

M. Binaghi, "Bollicine d'artista," in *Panorama*, 2 May

K. Iwakura, *M. Lodola*, Tokyo, June

T. Casetti, "Tutta mia soltanto mia," in *Casa Idea*, no. 27, 9 July

"Shoes Follies," in *Vogue Pelle*, October

G. Perretta, "You better move on Rolling Stones. Lodola," in *Paint it black*, exhibition catalogue, EOS Arte Contemporanea, Milan

Minestrone, exhibition catalogue, La Nuova Pesa, Rome

G. Perretta, "M. Lodola," in *Taxi-Art*

A. Bevilacqua, B. Pilat, *Artisti D.O.C.*, exhibition catalogue, Trent

R. Barilli, F. Capriccioli, *Il consumo disegnato*, exhibition catalogue, Rome

O. Calabrese, *A onor del falso*, exhibition catalogue, Rome

R. Restany, *Art & Tabac*, exhibition catalogue, Milan

F. Piquet, *Art is life*, exhibition catalogue

F. Fellini, S. Mazza, *Scarperentola*, exhibition catalogue, Milan

M. Carboni, "M. Lodola," in *Art Forum*

B. Munari, R. Margonari, V. Ronconi, *La plastica nell'arte*, exhibition catalogue, Verona

1994

S. Dell'Orso, "Un Milione," in *La Repubblica*, January

"M. Lodola nuovo futurista," in *La Repubblica*, 24 March

F. Frascione, in *Il Manifesto*, 8 April

E. Krumm, "M. Lodola Ritagli animati a due dimensioni," in *Corriere della Sera*, 10 April

M. Corgnati, F. Poli, *Dizionario d'Arte contemporanea*, Milan

V. Coen, C. Dehò, M. Deni, V. Tassinari, *Jambo–Jambo*, exhibition catalogue, Comune di Cesena

M. Francocci, exhibition catalogue for the Consigli di fabbrica, Spoleto; La Nuova Pesa, Rome

Ritratto Autoritratto, catalogue, Trevi

G. Nicoletti, "Nuovo futurismo," in *L'Adige*, 7 July

E. Boero, "Neo Futurismo," in *L'Arena*, 11 July

L. Serravalli, "Futuristi tutti in plastica," in *Alto Adige*, 17 July

"I giorni del Nuovo Futurismo," in *Vita Trentina*, 24 July

E. Maglia, "I protagonisti del Nuovo Futurismo al Museo Raveretano," in *La Provincia*, Cremona, 24 July

F. Krumm, "Reale, virtuale, praticamente un videogame," in *Corriere della Sera*, 24 July

C. Buzzi, "Così il futurismo torna a provocare," in *La Voce*, Mantua, 27 July

M.L. Bidonini, "Ecco il nuovo futurismo," in *La Nuova Venezia*, 28 July

G.M., "Agenda Elle," in *Elle*, August

A. Fiz, "Ritorno al futurista," in *Class*, no. 8, August

C. Spadoni, "Fanno bene a giocare i futuristi," in *Il Resto del Carlino*, 4 August

A. Masu, "Nuovo futurismo," in *Grazia*, 7 August

M. Campitelli, "Similcose di Neofuturismo,"

in *Il Piccolo*, 9 August

M.G. Fringuellini, "Nuovo Futurismo–L'arte si fa ironia plastificata," in *Il Giornale di Brescia*, 10 August

A. Nardi, "Il futurismo del futuro," in *Il Messaggero del Veneto*, 10 August

P. Bartellini, "Il nuovo futurismo è il trionfo del colore," in *Famiglia Cristiana*, no. 33, 17 August

R. Dallara, "Sulle orme di Depero, ma attenti al software," in *Il Giorno*, 17 August

G. Trevisan, "I nuovi futuristi odiano correre," in *L'Arena*, 25 August

R. Barilli, O. Calabrese, L. Pin, *Nuovo futurismo*, exhibition catalogue, Mart, Rovereto; Milan, in *Gente Mese*, no. 9, September

E. Pouchard, "Uno splendido disastro," in *La Gazzetta del Mezzogiorno*, 4 September

D. Auregli, "Neofuturismo," in *Il Manifesto*, 11 September

E. Crispolti, "La pittura in Italia," in *Il Novecento 3*, Milan

L. Cherubini, *Emergenze planetarie*, exhibition catalogue, Rome, Verona

A. Riva, "Nuovo futurismo," in *Donna Moderna*, 22 September

A. Marino, "Ritratto Autoritratto," in *Segno*, no. 136, October

E. Rizzoli, "Nuovo futurismo," in *Tema celeste*, no. 47–48

Zhao Gang, "Plastic dancing girls come to town," in *China Daily*, 30 November

"M. Lodola," in *Giornale del consumo cinese*, 3 December

M. Marosi, "Dalla Lombardia a Pechino sulla via dell'arte," in *L'Informazione*, 3 December

E. Tassini, "Lodola," in *L'Europeo*, no. 48, 7 December

A. Palermo, "Lodola," in *Beijing Youth Daily*, 12 December

M. Bonuomo, "Le silhouettes di Marco Lodola nella città proibita," in *Il Mattino*, 13 December

M. Gandini, "Punk o culturista, rappresento la mia vita," in *Il Giorno*, 28 December

Arte contemporanea italiana, no. 1, Milan

L. Meneghelli, "Nuovo futurismo," in *Flash Art*, no. 189, December–January

A.R. Brizzi, *Misure uniche per una collezione*, exhibition catalogue

G. Perretta, in *Art in Italy*, no. 2

E. Grazioli, *D'Altra parte*, ed. Bacacay

Arte in maschera, exhibition catalogue, Borgosesia (Vercelli)

P. Rampa, "La sottile arte del consumo," in *Il Manifesto*

A. Vettese, *Le tavole della legge*, exhibition catalogue, Castello di Volpaia

1995

A. Bassi, "Marco Lodola giovane futurista," in *Corriere Padano*, Piacenza, January

E. Concarotti, "A Piacenza è di scena il futurismo di Lodola," in *La Libertà*, Piacenza, 15 January

A. Chiappini, "Lodola. Leggerezza e trasparenza con il plexiglass," in *Il Giornale Nuovo*, 28 January

L. Somaini, C. Cerritelli, *Giovane arte contemporanea*, exhibition catalogue, Sartirana

M. Vescovo, *Marinetti e il movimento futurista*, exhibition catalogue, Palazzo Guasco, Alessandria

L. Somaini, C. Cerritelli, *Gioielli d'artista in Italia 1945–1995*, exhibition catalogue, Milan

D. Pano, "L'arte entra in bagno," in *Spazio casa*, October

F. Giorgi, "Acque d'autore," in *Gioia Arredamento*, October

M. Savio, "105 novità," in *Casaviva*, no. 10, October

M. Scotuzzi, "Tra arte e industria," in *Blu e Rosso*, October

S. Petricca, M. Francocci, *Marilyn Monroe*, exhibition catalogue, Milan, November

R. Mandrini, "Artisti pavesi in mostra a Roma," in *L'Indipendente*, 22 November

P.F. Damiani, *Il giorno e la notte, nuova poesia contemporanea,* Ragusa

F. Pratesi, E. Crispolti, *Un segno per il Sarno*, exhibition catalogue

C.M., "Simona Marchini presenta Lodola," in *La Gazzetta di Parma*, 2 December

P.E., "La zuppa pavese di Marco Lodola," in *La Tribuna di Parma*, 2 December

M.G. Villa, "Morirò dal ridere," in *La Tribuna di Parma*, 16 December

M. Garzonio, "Uomini, ecco il mio rifugio," in *La mia casa*, December–January

G. Carrano, in *Racconti legati*, Milan

R. Bossaglia, G. Perretta, A. Fiz, L. Mango, T. Conti, E. Pontiggia, *Nel segno dell'angelo*, exhibition catalogue, Milan

1996

S. Casciani, A. Mendini, C. Vannini, in *Louisiana Review*, Copenhagen, January

M.G. Villa, "Il flusso pavese di Lodola," in *La Tribuna di Parma*, 5 January

Il disegno italiano, no. 15, S. Polo d'Enza (Reggio Emilia)

W. Pagliero, "Illusioni allo specchio," in *Casa Oggi*, March

P. Schneidler, "Divorzio, parlano gli uomini," in *Gioia*, 16 March

"Gioielli d'autore," in *Vogue Gioiello*, April

R. Ciocca, B. Pilat, "Catalogo made in Art," in *Elle Decor*, April

M. Virgili, "Indossare l'arte," in *Amica*, 16 April

S. Mazza, C. Morozzi, *Imprevisto*, exhibition catalogue, Milan

L. Vergine, *L'arte in trincea*, ed. Skira

A. Boschi, "Questi piccoli indiani," in *La Provincia Pavese*, 6 July

D. Laboranti, *Appunti storici*, Dorno

M. Lodola, "Videofollie," in *La Repubblica*, Turin, 30 August

Lisa Parola, "Però che idee luminose," in *La Stampa*, Turin, September

P. Levi, "Il terzo futurismo di Lodola," in *La Repubblica*, 4 September

G. Ferrè, "Signori e signore," in *Io Donna, Corriere della Sera*, 7 September

A.M., "Arte musicale firmata Lodola," in *La Stampa*, 8 September

A. Boschi, "Marco Lodola. New York corteggia un futurista pavese," in *La Provincia Pavese*, 15 September

A. Fiz, "Futurismo al neon," in *Madame Class*, October

S. Varisco, A. Dominoni, "Espressioni artificiali," in *Gap Casa*, no. 130, October

A.M., "Pezzi di luce," in *Anna*, no. 41, 14 October

L. Praresi-L. Trucchi, *XII quadriennale*, exhibition catalogue, ed. De Luca

A. Riva, "Le sagome si riempiono di luce," in *Arte*, October

G. Curto, "Video follie di Lodola," in *Flash Art*, no. 200, November

"Marco Lodola in mostra alla Galleria Giulia," in *La voce repubblicana*, 26 November

F.M. Arisi Rota, "Incontri con l'artista," in *Tutto Vigevano*, December

A. Riva, "È nata la nuovissima avanguardia," in *Arte*, December

M. Zammamaro, in *Dire, Fare, Baciare. Smemoranda*, December

C. Cirinei, "Arte e spaghetti," in *Il Messaggero*, 6 December

V. Apuleo, "Voglia d'arte," in *Il Messaggero*, 9 December

R. Barilli, "Dal gotico al neon," in *L'Espresso*, 13 December

E. Di Martino, "Premio do forni XI ed.," in *Grafica Venezia*, 18 December

C. Squarcina, "A Pepper e Lodola il premio 'Do forni,'" in *La Nuova*, 19 December

A. Mammi, "Dai buttatevi nell'arte," in *L'Espresso*, 29 December

A. Boschi, "Lo scultore Lodola firma tazzine da caffè," in *La Provincia Pavese*

1997

Il Colbol (illustrations) January 95, Ata, Genoa

N. Lombardo, "Pinocchio e perspex a Valle Giulia," in *L'Unità*, 3 January

M. Mosana, "Risparmio e mercati," in *Il Sole 24 Ore*, 9 February

E. Concarotti, "Estroso gioco delle figurine," in *Libertà*, Piacenza, 27 February

M. Solbiati, "I giovani artisti? Apprendeteli al muro," in *Gulliver*, March

L. Giudici, in *Madrenatura*, exhibition catalogue, March, Prearo, Milan

E. Aldani, "Stregato dalla donna coccodrillo," in *La Provincia Pavese*, 1 March

D. Facchinetti, F. Lepore, "Mery en Mut," in *TV Sorrisi e canzoni*, no. 11, 16 March

D. Trento, "Lodola, rifacimenti e citazioni dell'esistente," in *La Repubblica*, 20 March

M. Chierici, "Parma dei desideri," in *Amica*, 21 March

M.P. Morani, *Racconti variopinti*, exhibition catalogue, Galleria Estense, Ferrara

L'Egitto, "Belle Arti," in *ViviMilano*, 27 March

E. Aldani, "L'artista in officina," in *La Provincia Pavese*, 30 March

Le opere di M. Lodola. Dentro Milano, March

A. Fiz, "Le altre copertine di Class," in *Class*, April

M. Moretti, "Nasce nel segno dell'arte la nuova città," in *Weekend Viaggi*, April

G. Chiappini, "Lodola, schermo strappato," in *La nuova Ferrara Arte*, 19 April

I. Saikako, cover illustration, Classici Feltrinelli (edited by Aldo Busi)

A. Fiz, in *Musicalmente*, exhibition catalogue, Galleria di Oggi, Biella, May

L. Magnetti, "Studenti di ieri e di oggi," in *Gioia*, no. 17, 3 May

Y.D., "Les sculpteurs en leur jardin," in *Nice-Matin*, 25 May

R. Barilli, "Poesia al neon," in *Quadri & sculture*, no. 25, April–May

J. Ceresoli, *M. Lodola*, Galleria Galvasina, Tema Celeste, no. 62, May–June

L. Maggi, "Giovani artisti a Torino," in *Elle Décor*, June

M.G. Torri, "Marco Lodola da Calvasina," in *Flash Art*, June–July

P. Bortolotti, "I gioiosi totem di Lodola," in *La Nazione*, 3 July

"Perspex al neon a Sarzana," in *Il Giornale dell'Arte*, no. 157, August

E. Di Mauro, *Va' pensiero*, exhibition catalogue, Turin

V. Coen, in *Univerarte*, exhibition catalogue, Bologna

M. Lodoli, *Diario di un millennio che fugge*, Einaudi

A. Zordan, "Va' pensiero," in *Marie Claire*, January

M.S. Metalli, *Libri-Babilonia*, no. 160, November

P. Marino, *Sirene a Polignano*, Segno, November–December

A. Busi, L. Cherubini, *Frames*, exhibition catalogue, Electa, Milan

M. Del Re, *Biennale Scultura*, exhibition catalogue, Montecarlo

P. Schneider, "Blind Date," in *Elle*, September

S. Morani, *Lodola. Il centro magico dell'umanità*, Economica, Pavia

U. Coen, *Traguardo*, exhibition catalogue, Galleria Colombo, Milan

R. Branà, *Sirene*, exhibition catalogue, Polignano al Mare (Bari)

F. Alcini, "Una carta telefonica," in *Cosmopolitan*, November

M. Gattermayer, "N.B.," in *Elle*, November

P. Rizzi, E. Di Martino, "Vetrina del nordest," in *Gazzettino di Venezia*, 15 September

A. Boschi, "Quelle sculture che luccicano," in *La Provincia Pavese*, August 3

A. Fiz, "In fiera a Napoli per l'arte del 2000," in *Carnet*, November

E. Loviro, "Esemplari intrecci moponici," in *Liberazione*, 4 May

O. Pedrini, "Si, un vizio ce l'hai," in *Tutto*, no. 12, December

"Il genio viene da nord," in *Class*, January

D. Liccardo, "Lodola," in *Next, Summer*

C. Desiata, "Per la forma," in *Come*, 6 June

O. Gambari, "Art café," in *La Repubblica*, Turin, 11 June

"Va' pensiero," in *Interni*, June

G. Piero Cane, "Virtù come gradevolezza," in *L'Unita*, 29 March

R. Perfettí, "M. Lodola da Ronchini," in *Next*, March

E. Aldani, "Ritratto da star," in *La Provincia Pavese*, 13 December

G. Ferrè, "Oggetti di passione," in *Io donna*, 13 December

D. Trombadori, "Dogmi da pluralisti," in *Quadri e sculture*, no. 28

A. Matarrese, "Periscopio," in *Panorama*, 19 December

P. Schneidler, "Aria di Natale," in *Elle*, December–January 1998

1998

G.M. Montesano, "La morte di Sissi," in *Flash Art*, February–March

L. Gattini, E. Lomuoio, *Inedito*, year 2, no. 1, Turin

M. Meneguzzo, *Due tre cose che sò di loro*, exhibition catalogue, Padiglione di Arte Contemporanea, Electa, Milan

S. Perazzoli, "E` di nuovo futurismo," in *Dove*, no. 12, February

This volume was printed by Elemond spa
at the plant in Martellago (Venice) in 1998